EVEN MORE

HORRIBLE
HISTORY

Thanks to Kath Mellentin for her extra research, help and cheerful advice

First published in 1997
by Macdonald Young Books

Macdonald Young Books, an imprint of
Wayland Publishers Ltd
61 Western Road
Hove
East Sussex
BN3 1JD

©1997 Macdonald Young Books

Find Macdonald Young on the internet
at http://www.wayland.co.uk

Commissioning editor: Debbie Fox

Design: The Design Works, Reading

Editor: Caroline Wilson

A CIP catalogue record for this book is
available from the British Library

ISBN: 0 7500 2177 2

Printed and bound in Portugal by
Edições ASA

EVEN MORE
HORRIBLE HISTORY

by **TIM WOOD**   illustrated by **IAN DICKS**

MACDONALD YOUNG BOOKS

To Charlotte and Laura Northedge
who provided so much inspiration for this book

Contents

Introduction

This book will not help you to pass history exams. It will be useless as a study guide and has almost no merit as a reference book. It is, simply, a tiny selection of the cornucopia of revolting and amusing bits of history which are mostly left out of other books (presumably to avoid offending good taste). Anyone of a nervous disposition should read no further.

Although many of the stories in this book are deliberately presented in an amusing way with the express aim of making you laugh, smile or be sick, approach them with caution. Most of the people in this book lived in a different time and place to us. Their beliefs and behaviour were different, and before we criticise them, we need to know more about the period in which they lived. In many ways we are not so much better than they were. War, torture, slavery and crime still exist. People still try dangerous cures and wear uncomfortable clothes. We have a long way to go before we can congratulate ourselves for being truly civilised. In fact it is quite likely that in 100 years, some other author will be electroscribing a CD with amusing stories about the ridiculous behaviour of people in the 1990s. And, no doubt, the horrible historians of 2100 will be having a good laugh at our expense. So watch out!

Last but not least, massacre, torture, murder, disembowelment, decapitation and the like as described in this book should be done only by trained experts. Please do not try any of these things yourself at home.

Food and Drink

There are basically two sorts of eaters – those who eat to live and those who live to eat. People who live to eat often don't actually live as long as the rest of us because they become very fat and die young. Happily for us, history is stuffed with large, wobbly, greedy people who astound us with their gargantuan appetites. Some of them made impressive marks on the pages of history because they exploded. You may be surprised to hear that William the Conqueror was an exploding fat person. As horrible historians we can also gag and retch when we read about people who revolt us by accident because they ate things which seem repulsive to us. But do remember that food is a matter of taste, and one person's roast leg of ant is another person's slug soup. Sometimes people eat odd things because they have no other choice. And who are we to criticise? Fried rat may be a delicious, crunchy snack – it is a natural food after all. Perhaps, like the Buckland family, we should try these things out for ourselves.

... and His Unfussy Father

Frank Buckland probably inherited his love of unusual food from his father, William Buckland. The two of them compete for the Horrible History title of Least Fussy Eater. Like his son, William also wanted to try everything. Among the foods he ate and enjoyed were alligator, mice on toast, and once even a portion of the embalmed heart of French King Louis XIV. Guests were probably very nervous indeed about being invited to the Buckland home because William expected them to eat everything he himself ate. Unlike his son, William never admitted he had eaten anything he did not like, although he did come close when he announced that he would probably not eat mole or stewed bluebottles if he was ever offered them again.

Exotic Eater...

One of the least fussy eaters must have been Frank Buckland, nineteenth-century author and naturalist. Buckland wanted to know what everything tasted like.

Among his more peculiar meals were elephant's trunk soup, roast giraffe and panther chops. He said that the only thing he did not like were earwigs, which tasted rather bitter.

Scorched Scoffers

The Ancient Greeks used their fingers to eat. One greedy Greek called Philoxenus spent hours hardening his fingers and gargling with near-boiling water so he could grab the tastiest morsels of food from the table before anyone else. When he had perfected this technique, other hungry diners started to accuse him of bribing the cooks to serve the food extra hot so that he could gobble it down before anyone else dared to take their first mouthful.

A Fishy Story

As an island, Britain has depended on a strong navy to defend its shores for hundreds of years. To make certain that there was always a good supply of trained sailors, Tudor monarchs encouraged the fishing industry by passing laws saying that on certain days of the week and at certain religious festivals, such as Lent, people had to eat fish instead of meat. People who failed to observe these 'Fish Days' were punished, usually by being placed in the pillory or stocks.

Blind Tasting

During the eighteenth century, most sailors ate with their eyes shut so they couldn't see what was on their plates. In the days before freezing, canning and other modern methods of preserving, food went bad on long voyages. Meat, which was salted in wooden barrels, went rotten and crawled with maggots. The water, which was stored in casks, went stale and smelt like water from a stagnant pond. The ship's biscuits were full of creepy-crawlies called weevils. Some sailors tapped their biscuits on the table before eating them, to knock out the weevils. Others just choked the biscuits down and thought of the weevils as extra meat!

8

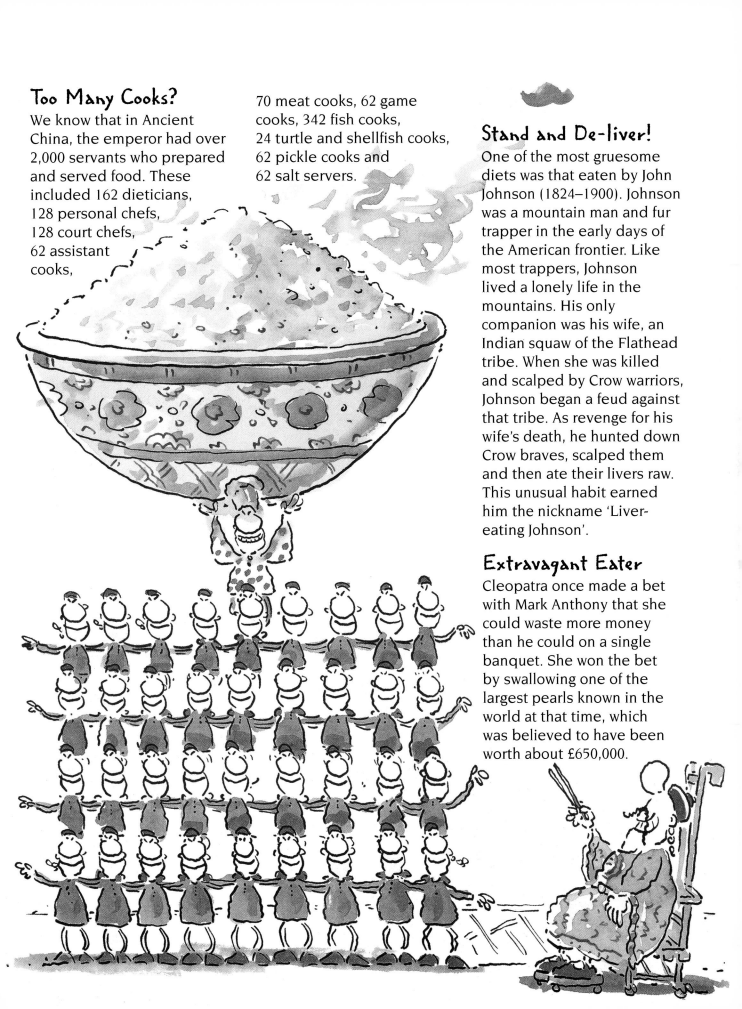

Too Many Cooks?

We know that in Ancient China, the emperor had over 2,000 servants who prepared and served food. These included 162 dieticians, 128 personal chefs, 128 court chefs, 62 assistant cooks, 70 meat cooks, 62 game cooks, 342 fish cooks, 24 turtle and shellfish cooks, 62 pickle cooks and 62 salt servers.

Stand and De-liver!

One of the most gruesome diets was that eaten by John Johnson (1824–1900). Johnson was a mountain man and fur trapper in the early days of the American frontier. Like most trappers, Johnson lived a lonely life in the mountains. His only companion was his wife, an Indian squaw of the Flathead tribe. When she was killed and scalped by Crow warriors, Johnson began a feud against that tribe. As revenge for his wife's death, he hunted down Crow braves, scalped them and then ate their livers raw. This unusual habit earned him the nickname 'Liver-eating Johnson'.

Extravagant Eater

Cleopatra once made a bet with Mark Anthony that she could waste more money than he could on a single banquet. She won the bet by swallowing one of the largest pearls known in the world at that time, which was believed to have been worth about £650,000.

Mind Your Manners!

During Medieval times, table manners were rather different from today. People ate with their fingers, often serving themselves from the same plates. Polite people were supposed to wash their hands before eating with other people. The 'Book of Curtesy' laid down some simple rules for cultured diners. Here are some of them:

- Don't play with cats or dogs at mealtimes
- Keep your nails clean
- Don't spit on the table
- If you blow your nose (there were no handkerchiefs of course) you should wipe your hands on your skirt or jacket afterwards
- Don't pick your teeth with a knife
- Don't clean your teeth with the tablecloth
- When you rinse out your mouth, don't spit back into the bowl (other people will need to use this water for rinsing!) but spit on the floor instead

Fishy Business

The Romans loved fish, and many rich Romans had their own fish farms. Mark Anthony's mother kept a favourite lamprey (a kind of eel) in hers, which, it was said, she adorned with gold earrings. One fish farmer, Vedius Pollio, was rumoured to have fed his prized fish on the flesh of dead slaves.

There She Blows

In Henry VIII's navy, sailors took pepper as a medicine to cure wind.

Shall I Cut it up for You?

Slaves cut up the food for rich Romans. They were called scissors.

Cruel Cabaret

The Roman Emperor Commodus was said to enjoy his meals most when prisoners were being torn to pieces in front of him.

Prehistoric pub

The longest-running restaurant in the world is Ma Yu Ching's Bucket Chicken House in Kaifen, China. It opened in 1153 and is still going strong, despite several changes of ownership. Let's hope they're not still serving the original food!

Body Matters

If we were to travel back into the past, we would immediately sense two striking differences from our own time – the dirt and the smell! In the past, hygiene and safe disposal of sewage and rubbish were not such high priorities as they are today. This meant that there was a lot more dirt around. As a result people did not smell very pleasant – and they never knew what they might step in, either! It is not quite true to say that nobody in the past noticed horrible smells because occasionally writers of the time commented on the vile stinks they encountered. Fortunately for us, we can only imagine what these must have been like. In addition, the odours and filth that clung to people in the past could easily hide the fact that they were suffering from some disgusting disease.

Mucky Monarch

If medals were given to monarchs for being anti-social, King James I would surely win a gold. Not only did he speak with a thick Scottish accent, which made him almost impossible to understand, but he also had a tongue which was too large for his mouth, so he slobbered uncontrollably. The danger of an unexpected spit bath kept many people at a distance. Those with delicate senses of smell were kept at bay by the fact that James had never bathed in his life. Several writers at the time commented on the strange, pudgy, grey colour of the king's skin. However, James was not completely unhygienic. When an emergency freshen-up was required, he would dip the tips of his fingers into a tiny bowl of rose water.

Coffin Chaos

During the sixth century, overcrowded graveyards became a major problem in Europe. Burial vaults inside churches were crammed with cracked and rotten coffins. During the summer the smell was revolting, and many churches suffered plagues of flies. Outside, coffins were buried on top of each other in the same holes. If they filled up the holes to ground level, more earth was shovelled on top. Sometimes, the ground level reached the window-sills. Mourners who didn't watch where they were walking could easily step on a rotten coffin lid and crash through layers of corpses.

Pretty Potty for a Royal Botty

Henry VIII ate a huge amount of food and, in order not to be inconvenienced, took his own portable toilet with him wherever he went. It was called a stool, and consisted of a large box with a lid and a potty inside. The box, including the feather-padded seat, was entirely covered in black velvet decorated with ribbons, fringes and 2,000 gold nails. The box had a large lock on it to prevent anyone but the king using it.

Catching Them with Their Trousers Down

Typhoid and dysentery, caused by drinking contaminated water, affected many armies in the Middle Ages. Often these diseases killed more soldiers than the enemy did or, at least, put entire armies out of action. During the Hundred Years War, hundreds of English archers were badly affected by diarrhoea. French soldiers soon learned that while a frontal attack could be dangerous, an assault from the rear was usually more effective. The French soon learned to be patient and bided their time when attacking. It was never long before the English soldiers had to squat and, with their pants down round their ankles, they were more or less helpless.

Thou Shalt not Bathe

During the Middle Ages, the Church condemned bathing except for those who were ill. One Christian pilgrim claimed that she had not washed her face for 18 years for fear of removing the holy blessing she received when she visited Jerusalem. Pope Gregory the Great did allow bathing on Sundays provided it did not become a 'time-wasting luxury'.

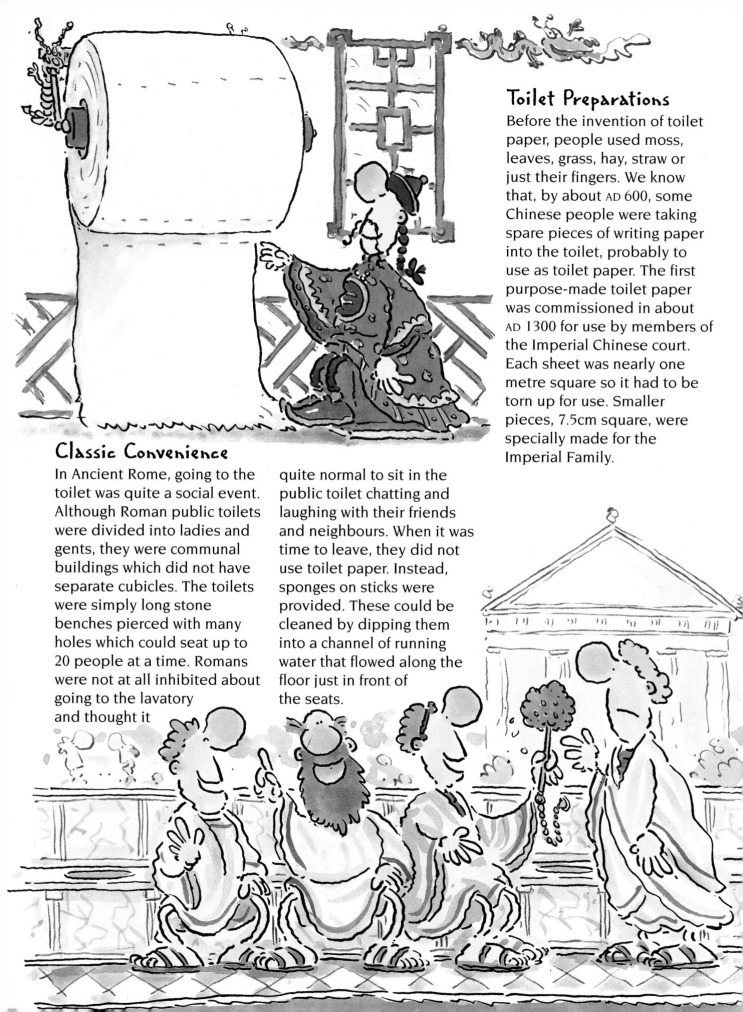

Toilet Preparations

Before the invention of toilet paper, people used moss, leaves, grass, hay, straw or just their fingers. We know that, by about AD 600, some Chinese people were taking spare pieces of writing paper into the toilet, probably to use as toilet paper. The first purpose-made toilet paper was commissioned in about AD 1300 for use by members of the Imperial Chinese court. Each sheet was nearly one metre square so it had to be torn up for use. Smaller pieces, 7.5cm square, were specially made for the Imperial Family.

Classic Convenience

In Ancient Rome, going to the toilet was quite a social event. Although Roman public toilets were divided into ladies and gents, they were communal buildings which did not have separate cubicles. The toilets were simply long stone benches pierced with many holes which could seat up to 20 people at a time. Romans were not at all inhibited about going to the lavatory and thought it quite normal to sit in the public toilet chatting and laughing with their friends and neighbours. When it was time to leave, they did not use toilet paper. Instead, sponges on sticks were provided. These could be cleaned by dipping them into a channel of running water that flowed along the floor just in front of the seats.

Breeding Like Rabbits

In 1726, Mary Toft of Godalming, England claimed that she had been attacked by a giant rabbit while out weeding. Her neighbours were surprised by this claim because they knew Mary to be a sensible woman, not given to flights of fancy. But the attack had taken place on St George's Day when, as everyone knew, supernatural forces were especially powerful. Mary gradually calmed down and, as time passed, most people forgot her weird story. Then, about five months later, Mary became very ill. She was examined by a local doctor who helped her give birth to five rabbits! Shortly after, the doctor, who had an excellent reputation, reported the birth of another seven rabbits! The news caused a sensation over the whole country and Mary's fame even spread to Europe. Doctors came from near and far to examine her. Mary gave birth to several more rabbits in front of them. Eventually, Sir Richard Manningham, an eminent physician, took Mary to London and, after keeping her under close supervision, announced that she was a fraud. Mary was arrested and confessed that her husband had been slipping her the rabbits when no one was looking so that she could produce them at the appropriate moment.

Roman Aroma Men

Although many Romans loved bathing, not all Romans smelled sweet. Writers at the time describe how the excited crowds at the arena gave off such sweaty odours and breathed out such stinking breath that cleaner members of the audience did not dare open their mouths for fear of breathing in poisoned air. On very hot days, slaves called sparsiones worked giant syringes to sprinkle perfume over the spectators in an attempt to sweeten the smell of the crowd.

Explosive Ending

In middle age, William the Conqueror became immensely fat. He was so fat that people used to laugh at him behind his back (which, of course, was very easy to do because he was so wide). William kept announcing his intention to go on a diet, but never quite got his act together. Then, in 1087, William led an attack on the town of Mantes. His army captured and burned the town. While William rode among the smoking ruins, his horse stepped on a burning ember and shied violently. This caused the iron pommel of William's saddle to strike the monarch violently in the stomach, rupturing his intestines and causing massive infection. William lay for five weeks in agonising pain until he finally died of festering internal abscesses. Unfortunately, the day of William's funeral was blisteringly hot. The king's body had putrified and swollen so much that when the church attendants lifted it from the bier, they found that it would not fit into the sarcophagus. They then had to try pressing on the king's stomach to push out the gas which was inflating his body. But they pressed just a bit too hard and William's stomach burst open. The assembled mourners raced from the church to escape the appalling stench, with hands clapped over their noses. The Bishops, unable to close the coffin lid completely, conducted one of the fastest royal funeral services on record!

All Washed Up

In about 1800, the 11th Duke of Norfolk, an enormously fat man, could drink far more than anyone else without showing any signs of drunkenness. However, when he eventually had drunk too much, he simply became paralysed. At this point, his servants would rush forward, lift the Duke on to a stretcher and carry him off. While the Duke was unconscious, the servants took the opportunity to undress him and wash him all over. As the Duke hated the sight of water and refused to wash himself, this was the only chance his household had to get him clean.

Waterloo Portaloo

Potties or jerries have always been useful portable toilets. During the 1800s, decorated potties became very popular. During the wars against France, patriotic people got a lot of satisfaction out of using potties which had portraits of Napoleon painted in them. In this way they could really show what they thought of the enemy! Another popular model of potty had a large eye in the bottom with the rhyme, 'Use me well and keep me clean, and I'll not tell what I have seen'.

Old Habits Die Hard

Scraps of cloth found in toilet pits in certain monasteries, such as that at St Albans, England, suggest that before the invention of toilet paper, the monks used pieces of cloth torn from old habits.

Nasty Jobs

However rich a society may be, somebody has to do those really horrible jobs which we prefer not to think about – not when we're eating, anyway! Someone has to dispose of the sewage, the rubbish, the dead bodies and those ghastly, smelly, rotting, slimy, lumpy things. Luckily, there are always a few people who, for the right price, will do practically anything. They are the unsung heroes and heroines of history, without whom none of the other horrors which we enjoy reading about so much would have been possible. These people think nothing of standing up to their waists in nastiness while they shovel something offensive into a loathsome pit. Let's hope they washed their hands before they picked their noses.

Pirate Short-Cut

Being a pirate must have been one of the nastiest jobs – all that fighting and drinking to be done. But most pirates were very lazy. Blackbeard, for example, never bothered to search his victims. He simply seized hold of a prisoner who was wearing a large ring and then cut off his or her finger to get the loot. This was brutal, but it saved a lot of work because, as soon as the other prisoners saw what had happened, they rushed forward enthusiastically to offer all their personal possessions to the pirate before he could repeat the dreadful process.

Is There Life After Death?

Dr Guillotin was sure that victims executed by guillotine felt only a slight chill caused by the wind of the falling blade before they died, and that death was instantaneous. Others were not so sure, and rumours spread that heads had smiled and even talked after death. Doctors and medical students crowded round scaffolds, grabbing fresh heads as they were cut off and subjecting them to all kinds of experiments. They stuck pins in the lips, applied smelling salts to the nose, and singed the eyeballs with candle flames. Some claimed that they saw reactions but others remarked drily that they saw only looks of astonishment.

Wanted – One Hermit...

Eighteenth-century landowner Charles Hamilton redesigned his garden with artificial hills and valleys, temples and grottoes, and a vast new lake. The only thing missing was a hermit! So he advertised for one. On the face of it, the job sounded very simple and no previous experience was required. But when the new hermit found out that he was not allowed to wash or cut his hair, leave the garden at any time, or talk to anyone (including the servants who brought his food), and that he had to wear itchy clothes made of animal hair, he couldn't stand it. Three weeks after his arrival, he escaped into the night and was never seen again.

Buffalo Bother

Before the coming of European settlers to the American West, the Great Plains thronged with gigantic herds of buffalo. There may have been as many as 70 million of these magnificent animals. The Plains Indians depended on the buffalo, hunting it and using every part of it – they ate the meat and used the skin to make clothes and tents. However, during the 1880s, professional and sporting hunters virtually wiped out the buffalo herds. One of the most famous hunters, Buffalo Bill, killed 69 in a single day during a contest with another hunter, William Comstock. The first hunters were hired by the railroads to supply meat for their workers. But after the railroads were built, the hunters took only the buffalo hides. After they had skinned their prey, they left the rest of the carcass to rot in the sun. It is said that buffalo carcasses lined 200 miles of track along the Kansas Pacific railroad.

Wanted for Rustling

Faced by the constant danger of being shot in the back or challenged to a shoot-out by someone with a faster draw, many gunslingers in the Wild West adopted the tactics of shooting first and asking questions later. One of the fastest and least chatty gunslingers was Wild Bill Hickok. In one shoot-out, while acting as law officer in the wild cowtown of Abilene, trigger-happy Hickok gunned down not only the lawbreaker but also his own deputy. Eventually, Hickok became so terrified of being ambushed that he scattered crumpled pieces of newspaper round his bed while he slept so that he could hear anyone who tried to creep up on him.

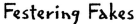

Festering Fakes

Bogus beggars often try to get sympathy by exhibiting ghastly pretend sores or wounds. During Victorian times, one trick was to cover a patch of skin with a layer of soap and then apply strong vinegar. This created what appeared to be large, yellow, pus-filled blisters. Another good trick was to place a piece of raw meat on a limb and bandage it so that some of the meat showed through, looking like a open sore.

Pipe Cleaners

A hundred and fifty years ago, sewer cleaning was one of the most disgusting jobs. According to an 1848 report, London sewer cleaners could expect to find 'the ingredients from the breweries, the gas-works, and the several chemical and mineral manufactories; dead dogs, cats, kittens, and rats; offal from slaughterhouses, sometimes even including the entrails of the animals; street-pavement dirt of every variety; vegetable refuse; stable-dung; the refuse of pig-styes; night-soil; ashes; tin kettles and pans; broken stoneware, glass jars, pitchers, flower-pots etc.; bricks; pieces of wood; rotten mortar and rubbish of different kinds; and even rags'. The rotting muck could give off deadly gases, and sewer cleaners were often overcome by poisonous fumes.

Bottled B.O.

In the 1780s, an Italian scientist called Canon Gattoni set out to discover how smelly beggars were. He hired suitable volunteers and put them into huge leather sacks which were fastened tightly round their waists. After leaving them for some time in order that they should give off horrid smells and odours, he collected the stale air from the sacks by means of large funnels and stored it in glass bottles ready for his stinky experiments.

An 'Eye Risk' Job

You may think that eye operations are comparatively new. In fact doctors carried them out in Ancient Babylonia nearly 3,000 years ago. We know this because laws were passed at that time which fixed the fees a doctor could charge for performing the operation. The operations seem to have been nearly as risky for the doctor as for the patient, though. If a doctor blinded a slave, he had to provide the owner with a new, healthy slave. But if the doctor blinded a wealthy patient, he had his hand cut off.

Yankee Diddle Dandy

During the American Civil War, soldiers were paid a bounty to enlist in the Union Army. Thousands of young men were proud to join and fight for a cause in which they believed. But others saw this as an excellent way to make money. These men enlisted, took the bounty, then deserted and re-enlisted somewhere else to get a second bounty. One fast-moving soldier was found to have enlisted 32 times. We now know that there were several well-organised gangs of these 'Bounty Jumpers'. One gang was organised by a gambler, Mike McDonald, who controlled the movements of his bogus soldiers like a military campaign, moving flags on a giant map to keep track of their activities. As many as half of all the desertions from the Union army – about 135,000 – were probably the result of bounty jumping.

Pop Goes the Wee Cell

Being a plumber in 1814 could be quite dangerous. A Mr Phair, writing about toilets, described two plumbers who went to repair a blocked lavatory. Unknown to them, explosive gases from decomposing sewage had gathered under the floor. When they lifted the flagstone and lit a candle to peer into the pit, the gas exploded, setting one man on fire and knocking out the other.

Foul Fashions

Just as you should never judge a book by its cover, so you should never judge people by the clothes they wear. Throughout history people have worn what seem to us to be the most ridiculous and uncomfortable clothes. They seem willing to suffer torment worse than any medieval torture just to look fashionable. But once again, we should not be too quick to criticise fashions of the past. Just as our parents cringe with embarrassment at old photos of them wearing flares and platform soles, so you will blush with shame in a few years when you see videos of yourselves dressed in what you now think is the height of fashion.

Scratch 'n Sniff

King James I was terrified of assassination, so he wore heavy, padded, dagger-proof doublets. But the king also liked a good scratch. He had his doublets decorated with extravagant slits so he could reach inside and scratch the itches made by the fleas and lice which infested his body.

Stripping for Action

Born in 1796, Squire Jack Mytton loved sports. Horse racing and hunting were his favourites. He fought dogs and bears with his teeth. He drove his carriage at reckless speed, once overturning it in a ditch just to show a friend what a crash felt like. Jack was also famous for his huge wardrobe which contained 3,000 shirts, 1,000 hats, 700 pairs of riding boots and 150 pairs of breeches. In spite of having all these clothes, when Jack went shooting he wore only a linen jacket, silk stockings and thin shoes. Sometimes, in spite of gales and snow, he was so overcome with the thrill of the chase that he threw off all his clothes and chased ducks through the icy marshes stark naked.

Hair Today, Gone Tomorrow

Everyone thought that Mary Queen of Scots had a fine head of red hair. But after her execution, the headsman went to lift up her head by the hair. At that moment he discovered that he was holding only a wig, and could only watch in horror as her head bounced off the floor with a loud thud.

Mean Minister

Morgan Jones, Vicar of Blewbury from 1781-1824, was a great miser. One saving he made was that he never changed his clothes. Morgan repaired his worn-out black hat with the brim of a hat he stole from a scarecrow – although it was brown. He wore the same overcoat, hat and shirt throughout his ministry. Whenever his coat became too worn, he patched it, darned it, turned it inside out, and repaired it with yarn borrowed from his parishioners – whatever colours they would give him. The patched coat of many colours is still preserved in a glass case and can be seen to this day.

Beauty Ban

Cosmetic face packs were condemned by the early Church as 'poultices of lust'.

Curious Costumes

During the reign of Queen Victoria, Lady Cardigan was famous for her odd clothes. She went cycling in red trousers and a leopardskin cape. She wore extravagant ball gowns and danced wild Spanish dances while playing the castanets. She often walked in Hyde Park in fancy dress. Her most curious costume was a coffin. She kept this at home, and would lie in it from time to time in order to try it on for size.

Boil in the Bag

One of the strangest garments must have been the 'bath bag' invented by Doctor Sanctorius, an Italian doctor who died in 1636. This was a huge waterproof bag that a patient could sit in. Water was poured in through a funnel at the neck so that the patient could lie in the bag and soak. When the bath was over, the water was allowed to run away through a drain at the foot of the bag. A later, improved version of 1898 was made of rubber and had rubber arms with gloves at the end so the patient could hold a newspaper or sip a drink while enjoying the bath!

Given a Wigging

Wigs are not new fashion accessories. Many Roman women wore wigs. Some bald Roman men wore them too, although those who were not rich enough to afford these expensive items simply painted false hair on their heads! However, wig-wearing lost popularity after Rome was conquered. This was partly because the early Christian Church opposed wigs, saying that when the priest laid hands on a wig-wearer, God's blessing could not penetrate the false hair! In 1692, the Council of Constantinople actually excommunicated Christians for wearing wigs.

A Cure for Smoking

Sir Walter Raleigh is thought to have been the first European to bring tobacco from America. On one occasion, shortly after his return to England, Sir Walter lit a pipe of tobacco to have a peaceful smoke. His servant, never having seen a pipe smoked before, thought that this master had caught fire. He promptly threw a jug of ale over Sir Walter to put out the fire!

All Change!

Martial, the Roman poet, wrote of one host who was so vain and fashion-conscious that during one meal, he changed his clothes no less than eleven times, using the great heat as his excuse.

Fizzy Footgear

George 'Beau' Brummel was extremely fussy about his clothes and would spend hours getting dressed. He liked his boots to look immaculate and required his servants to polish them with champagne froth – even on the soles.

Wrapping Up Warmly

US President Zachary Taylor may have been killed by his clothes. The President took part in Independence Day ceremonies in Washington in 1850 wearing a black suit and a high, stiff collar. The weather was fiercely hot and the President was seen to be sweating throughout the long ceremonies. He became faint and later collapsed with stomach cramps and a high fever. Doctors were unable to bring Taylor's temperature down and a few days later, he died. Modern opinion is that he had suffered acute sunstroke caused by overheating in unsuitable clothes and may have been helped along by drinking contaminated water.

Handlebar Halter

During the Victorian period, moustaches became very fashionable. In 1873, Eli Randolph of New York patented a moustache guard. The guard was made of rubber and was held in place by two curved prongs which were inserted into the nostrils. The maker claimed that not only did his guard protect the moustache from becoming soiled with food and drink, but it also made kissing easier and more hygienic.

Colour Blind

During the Regency days, men took fashion very seriously and spent hours preparing themselves for outings. Henry Cope of Brighton set a new trend by wearing only green. All his clothes were green – right down to the buttons on his waistcoat. His carriage, jewellery, luggage, riding whip and gloves were all green. The rooms in his home were painted green. And although his wig and face were powdered white, reflected light made his skin and hair look green. Not surprisingly, he became known as the 'Green Man of Brighton'.

X-Ray Vision

When X-rays were first discovered in 1895, a rumour developed that it would soon be possible to produce X-ray spectacles. Taking advantage of this, one company started to manufacture underwear that was guaranteed to be X-ray proof.

Toupee or not Toupee

The Ancient Egyptians could never make up their minds whether hair was a good or bad thing. On the one hand, they believed that hair was unclean and shaved it from their heads and every other part of their bodies. On the other hand, no self-respecting Egyptian would be seen dead without a wig. And all Pharaohs, whether male or female, wore ceremonial false beards.

Pampered Poppaea

One of the most pampered women in history must have been Poppaea, the wife of the Roman Emperor Nero. She had no less than one hundred female attendants. They helped her put on her face mask of bean meal, take her daily bath in ass's milk, cover her body with poisonous white-lead cream, paint her cheeks with red paint and her eyebrows with black antimony, pick out her veins with blue paint, and clean her teeth with pumice powder.

Beady-Eyed

The Mayans thought that being cross-eyed was a sign of great beauty. Parents hung beads from bands round their children's foreheads to encourage them to go cross-eyed. Being cross-eyed obviously gave the Mayans a strange view of the world because they also thought that having flat foreheads was a sign of great beauty! In order to achieve this effect, Mayan parents would strap boards to their baby's head to mould the soft skull bone into the correct shape.

Goldilocks

Wigs were important fashion accessories in Ancient Rome. Blond and red hair from Germany was the most popular. At one time, a wig made from German hair cost its own weight in gold.

Crazy Inventions

Luckily for those of us who are interested in the odder and more amusing aspects of the past, history is packed with crackpots and weird inventors. These oddballs have devised a huge variety of crazy contraptions which are either horrible or hilarious and, in some cases, both. Some of the most repulsive inventions include new weapons of death, novel methods of extermination and fresh instruments of torture. These devices could be literally side-splitting. Other inventions seem, at first sight, to benefit humankind but, fortunately for us, can also, entirely by accident, create abominable or amusing consequences. Here is a selection of a few of the more bizarre and revolting.

The Life and Soul of the Party

During the Middle Ages, people discovered that a body could be preserved much longer if the internal organs were removed at death. This new practice of 'evisceration' actually made it possible for Pedro I of Portugal, to have his dead girlfriend, Inès de Castro, crowned as his queen when he ascended to the throne. Pedro ordered Inès, who had been murdered two years earlier in 1355, to be brought out of her magnificent tomb and propped up on the throne, wearing a crown and richly embellished robes of state. Many nobles and clergy paid homage to their new queen by kneeling in front of her and kissing her (rather bony) hand. Inès graciously accepted their tributes before taking part in the coronation feast. A mere shadow of her former self, Inès sat quietly through the banquet, although she did not seem to enjoy the food much and ate very little. When the feasting was over, Inès returned to her tomb at the head of a royal procession, happily riding in a chariot drawn by six black mules. Without the invention of evisceration, none of this would have been possible.

Watch Your Step

The Chinese were probably the first people to invent landmines. In 1277, they used their first mine which was exotically named 'The Underground Sky-Soaring Thunder' against invading Mongols. The mine was basically a booby trap. It was hidden under a group of spears and banners stuck in the ground, which looked like tempting trophies for the Mongols. As the enemy soldiers advanced to capture the trophies, they stepped on a buried trigger which lit the fuse. This set off a gunpowder bomb whose explosion drastically rearranged the landscape and anybody standing on it.

Tanks for the Memory

The first tanks were probably invented by the Assyrians 3,000 years ago. These ruthless warriors built six-wheeled siege engines, each sheathed in wickerwork to protect the crew. A huge battering ram or twin giant lances stuck out of the front to attack the enemy. Inside was a large water tank, the contents of which was used to put out the flames if the vehicle caught fire. The tanks were used with devastating effect against city walls.

An Unusual Angle

During the late eighteenth century, librarian Thomas Birch, who was a fanatical fisherman, hit on the bright idea of fooling the fish by disguising himself as a tree. He made a costume with artificial branches and covered his rod with blossoms. We don't know whether he caught any fish, but he caused so much amusement among his colleagues, who called him 'Thomas the Birch Tree', and such terror among riverside ramblers who stumbled unexpectedly across him, that he decided to give up his tree disguise before someone chopped him down to size.

Claw Blimey!

When the Romans attacked Syracuse in 215 BC, they expected an easy victory. They brought siege towers tall enough to top the city walls and a catapult which was so big that it had to be carried on a platform made of eight ships lashed together. But thanks to the genius of Archimedes, the Roman war machine was stopped in its tracks. The scientist had invented giant cranes, called the 'Claws of Archimedes' which plucked the Roman ships out of the water and smashed them on the rocks, as well as giant catapults which rained huge stones down on the legions. The Romans were terrified and made little progress in their siege until, while the inhabitants were distracted by a festival of feasting, they managed to force their way into the city on foot.

Chopping List

Contrary to popular belief, Dr Guillotin did not invent the guillotine, he only recommended it as a more humane form of execution. Historians now think about 2,500 people were executed by this machine during the French Revolution. According to legend, one of them was Dr Guillotin. Sadly this is not so. He died in bed at the age of 76 of an infected carbuncle on his shoulder.

Fresh Air Fiend

Thomas Thorneycroft was one of those great Victorian inventors who designed a number of completely useless gadgets. He designed strap-on wings and arranged for his butler to try them out by jumping off the roof. Unfortunately, the wings were not very effective and instead of soaring gracefully over the garden, the butler plummeted into a rhododendron bush. Thomas continued to be interested in the twin themes of air and movement, however. A great believer in the benefits of fresh air, he had over 60 ventilators built into his family home at Tottenhall Towers. His crowning achievement was to draw up a magnificent plan for piping bracing air from the seaside directly into homes in London. Sadly, like his flying butler, the scheme crashed.

An Old Banger

In 1425, an Italian engineer called Giovanni di Fontana drew a design for a rocket car. The car was basically a wooden platform on two rollers. The rocket motor was powered by a secret fuel consisting mainly of gunpowder. As far as we know, the car never ran. If it had, the resulting explosion would probably have destroyed all evidence of its existence.

Bad Breath

The gas chamber was introduced as a quicker and more humane method of execution than the electric chair. In fact it is anything but. The average length of time it takes a victim to die is eight minutes. The longest death on record is 11 minutes. The main reason for this is that victims are told to inhale the gas deeply so they will die quickly and painlessly. But when a victim breathes in the first lungful of gas, the body instinctively recognises the gas as not being air and refuses to breathe in more.

Get the Point?

The first 'machine gun' was invented by Dionysus of Alexandria in AD 100. It consisted of an immense multi-firing catapult which had a magazine of large arrows. The machine could fire the arrows one after the other but, once the firing had started, the aim could not be altered. The Chinese improved on this when they invented a rapid-fire crossbow about 1,000 years later. This could be held in the hand. Test firings have shown that 100 soldiers armed with the weapon could fire 2,000 arrows in 15 seconds over a range of about 80 metres. To make the weapon even more effective, the arrows were poison-tipped.

Maritime Monster

Rulers always like to have bigger and better weapons than their enemies. King Hiero of Syracuse (270-215 BC) was no exception. He built a super ship powered by 20 banks of oars. It had several armoured turrets which protected cranes designed to drop stones on, and grapple with, other ships, and a giant catapult. Over 200 marines worked the weapons. The ship, which was called the Syracusa, had a freshwater tank that held 91,000 litres of drinking water; a huge seawater tank for holding fish; stables for 20 horses; numerous storerooms; a flour mill; a gymnasium; a bathroom containing three bronze bath tubs; a temple; flowerbeds; and a library. We don't know how large the crew was (although a similar Egyptian ship had 4,000 oarsmen!), but we do know the Syracusa had its own law court on board.

Megaphonic Messages

The Ancient Romans developed lots of clever ways of signalling, including beacon fires, flags and a postal service. But when Julius Caesar invaded Gaul (modern France) he was very impressed with the system used by Gallic tribes to telegraph messages to each other. The Gauls simply shouted loudly. In this way messages were passed from field to field, village to village, tribe to tribe and, in a remarkably short time, right across Gaul. It is estimated that messages shouted in this way could travel at about 20 kilometres per hour.

Fire Fighting

The first use of flamethrowers in war came in AD 674 when a Syrian chemist called Callanicus invented a substance called 'Greek Fire'. The exact composition of this hideous stuff is not known but it probably contained sulphur, saltpetre, oil or perhaps gasoline, and resin to hold everything together in a sticky ball of fire. It was either shot in a flaming ball from a catapult or squirted over enemy ships through a pump.

Water Wonder

Have you ever used a dispensing machine? Did you know that these were invented by the Ancient Greeks nearly 2,000 years ago? Greek dispensing machines were kept in temples. A coin dropped in the machine would tip a small lever which opened a valve. This served a small quantity of water through a tap so the user could wash his or her hands and face before going to worship.

Cooling Crown

Sir Francis Galton, the Victorian inventor of fingerprinting, had a mortal fear that his brain might overheat. To avoid this possibility he designed a hat which contained several tiny shutters. He operated these ventilators by pressing a bulb on the end of a rubber tube. This caused the shutters to spring open so cooling breezes could flow across his cranium.

Getting to the Bottom of it

Sir Francis Galton was also fascinated by the different races of people in the world and made a study of them. As part of his researches he became very interested in the size of African ladies' bottoms. Realising that he could not simply walk up to a strange lady and clap a tape measure to her posterior, he devised a way of investigating backsides from a distance. This involved taking measurements with a sextant in very much the same way as a modern surveyor would measure the landscape to plot the route of a new motorway. Galton then translated his surveying measurements with geometry and mathematical tables into the actual dimensions of the distant behind.

Crime and Punishment

Without rules there would be chaos in most societies. Some might argue that even with rules, there is a fair degree of chaos because humans often object to being told what to do and refuse to co-operate with the authorities. In ancient times, rulers believed that the punishments they used to enforce their laws had to be cruel in order to terrify criminals and so prevent them from committing crimes. This is the reason why, in the past, criminals were flogged, tortured, mutilated, executed and otherwise treated harshly for what seem to us to be quite minor offences – such as stealing a lamb.

But, of course, while there are laws there will always be lawbreakers. Vicious punishments do not necessarily stop determined criminals. People like this think that if they are going to be hanged for stealing a lamb they might as well steal a sheep as well – not to mention killing the farmer and his family, burning down the farmstead, thus setting fire to the town, and accidentally killing the king's only son, so starting a fierce civil war which lasts for 25 years, costing 3,000 lives and bringing untold misery to the whole population.

Curious Crimes

Crimes that carry the death penalty have varied considerably throughout history. In ancient times, people could be executed for singing insulting songs and making a noise after dark in Rome; for killing a cat in Egypt; for stealing a royal elephant in India; for cursing in Judea; for selling bad beer in Babylon; and for giving a bad haircut in Assyria!

Cooking a Cook

Henry VIII introduced an unusual method of execution in 1531 – boiling alive. The first victim of this new punishment was a cook, Richard Roose, chef to the bishop of Rochester. Richard was accused of poisoning members of the bishop's household when six of them became ill and two died after eating a meal he had cooked. Richard was put in a pot that was hung from a tripod in the town square at Smithfield. It took two hours for the water in the pot to come to the boil. This awful method of punishment was allowed for only 16 years. It was withdrawn by Henry's son, Edward VI, when his father died.

34

The Full Weight of the Law

In Medieval England, one of the worst sorts of punishment – pressing to death – was invented more or less by accident. In 1275, it was decided that people who refused to be tried either by a jury or in a trial by battle should be put 'en le prison forte et dure' (in strong and hard prison). At first this meant being locked up for a year and a day in the worst part of the prison. But eventually – no one knows exactly how – the word 'prison' was replaced by the word 'peine' meaning pressure. Prisoners sentenced to 'peine forte et dure' were spreadeagled and chained to the floor of their dungeon. The executioner placed a flat board across the victim's chest and piled rocks, chains and weights on top. The weights were added one at a time, making it hard for the victim to breathe, but taking care that life was not extinguished too soon. The executioner was instructed to make the victim suffer for as long as possible. A skilled executioner could keep a victim alive, but in agony, for many days by adding the weights very slowly and feeding him bread and water.

Child Smokers

The Aztecs didn't believe in smacking their children. Instead, they punished badly-behaved offspring by pricking them with sharp sticks, and holding them over the smoke of a fire to make them cough out the badness.

Flying Tonight

One of the most unusual forms of execution ever devised was 'death by flying'. This was invented by the Chinese Emperor Kao Yang. The Emperor was studying to be a Buddhist, which meant that he was not allowed to harm living creatures and, in fact, was supposed to free trapped animals. Kao Yang wanted to bump off all rivals to the throne, but his Buddhist principles would not allow him to harm them. He had his prisoners brought one by one to the top of a high tower where they were fitted with wings made of bamboo matting. Kao Yang ordered his prisoners to fly to freedom. Then, roaring with laughter, he watched them plunge to their deaths. We know that he killed over 700 rivals in this way in a single year.

Fire-Fighting Fraudsters

Fires were common in Ancient Rome and, although there was a public fire-fighting force, it was not very efficient. The firefighters were slaves and, unwilling to expose themselves to unnecessary danger, they were often slow to respond to emergencies. This created an opportunity for unscrupulous citizens such as one called Crassus who had his own private firefighters. When there was a fire, Crassus and his team would arrive on the scene. He would then set about buying all the houses near the fire. If owners refused to sell, Crassus' team would make no effort to fight the fire. As the flames rose higher, Crassus made lower and lower bids until the owners sold. Only then would Crassus' team step in to put out the fires in his newly bought houses.

Keeping Them on Their Toes

Some of the most brutal characters in history were pirates. Pirate captains lived outside the law and they had no police or public disapproval to control their cruelty. Many pirates were deliberately cruel simply to terrify their own cut-throat crews into unthinking obedience. Blackbeard, for example, once shot his first mate Israel Hands in the knee while playing cards for no reason at all. The wounds left Hands lamed for life. Blackbeard afterwards explained that he had to do something like that to the crew every now and again to put them off doing the same thing to him.

Quick on the Snore

One of the most notorious gunslingers of the Wild West was John Wesley Hardin. It is claimed that he had more than 40 notches cut in his gun handle – one for each of the men he killed. Hardin, who was a lawyer, was quick-tempered and arrogant. Once, when staying in a hotel, he was disturbed by the sound of a man snoring in the next room. After a few minutes of irritable tossing and turning, he simply got up, took his gun, went to the next room and shot the man dead!

What a Shocking Waste

In the 1890s, the Emperor of Ethiopia learned that the electric chair had become the newest method of execution in the USA. He immediately ordered three electric chairs to be sent to his palace. But the Emperor was more than a little upset when he realised that the chairs needed electricicity to work and, unfortunately, there was no electricity in Ethiopia at that time! But the chairs were not entirely wasted. The Emperor used one as a throne, thus demonstrating that not even the latest technology could harm him.

The Painful Truth

Torture reached its peak between the mid-fourteenth and mid-eighteenth centuries, when it was the approved method of questioning political and religious prisoners. The top three torture instruments used at that time were the rack, the strappado and the thumbscrew. The rack was a table for stretching the victim's limbs and body. The strappado consisted of a crane which hoisted the victim's weighted body by a rope fastened to his hands, which were tied behind him.

The thumbscrew was a metal vice used to grip and crush the victim's thumbs or fingers.

Other favourite torture devices and methods included the boot (like a large thumbscrew which tightened on, and finally crushed, the foot) and the bastinado – a frame for tying the victim's bare feet while the soles were beaten with rods. Something a little bit different was the water torture, where a funnel was pushed down the victim's throat and water poured into it in order to stretch the stomach.

Arguments, Quarrels and Worse

Humans have fought each other for as long as they have been on Earth – and they will probably continue to do so until we are all extinct. Sometimes, even when there is really no reason for a quarrel, people will make one up. This was how the War of Jenkin's Ear began – fought because a sailor had his ear cut off! Sadly, quarrels and arguments between rulers usually end up with a lot of ordinary folk getting hurt. This might be entertaining for us to read about long after the event, but it was not much fun for the people concerned. So spare a thought for the millions of people who just wanted to lead simple existences with their families, but ended up giving their lives to help settle arguments between ambitious rulers.

Wicked Stepmother

King Edward the Martyr (963–978) had one of those cruel stepmothers we love to hate. Queen Alfthryth wanted her own nine-year-old son, Athelred, to be king instead of Edward. When Edward made an informal visit to his stepmother's castle without his bodyguard, she seized her chance to kill the teenage king. Treacherously she offered Edward a welcome cup then, as he tipped his head back to drink, she grabbed his arms while her servants rushed up and stabbed him to death.

A Royal Rumble

One of the most unlikely causes for war occurred in Ancient Egypt in about 1580 BC when King Apophis of Upper Egypt sent a message to King Sekenenre of Lower Egypt which went something like this: 'The farting of the hippopotami swimming in the sacred temple pool at your palace is keeping me awake. Do something about it, or else!' Sekenenre knew an insult when he saw it, after all, Apophis' bedroom was over 640 kilometres away!

He promptly declared war. Sekenenre was killed in the war, but his son carried on the fight. Apophis died of stress when he realised that he was going to lose the 'War of the Hippo Farts'.

Mongol Mayhem

The Mongols were fierce nomadic people who were renowned for their cruelty. Among their cruellest leaders was Tamerlane the Great. When rebellious Persians massacred some of his soldiers, Tamerlane ordered their execution. His soldiers worked hard chopping off heads. When Tamerlane rode away, he left behind a pyramid of 70,000 skulls heaped outside the city walls.

Toilet Terror

King Edmund Ironside had one of the most horrible ends in the whole of human history – killed as he went to the toilet! Unknown to the king, one of his enemies had hidden in the dung pit. As Edmund crouched over the pit to answer nature's call, the hidden assassin stabbed upwards with a long dagger. He must have been able to see what he was doing (yecch!) because he scored a bullseye! Leaving his dagger firmly lodged in his victim's vitals, the assassin hopped out of the pit and ran off. Edmund died in agony shortly afterwards. Edmund's friends were soon hot on the scent of the assassin, who was eventually caught and killed – presumably from a considerable distance.

Fling Dung Merrily on High

The Chinese invented poison gas bombs and smoke bombs. But perhaps the worst of all their bombs was the excrement bomb. This was described in AD 1044, by Tseng Kung-Liang in his Military Encyclopaedia. The bomb was made from human excrement mixed with various chemicals. The mixture was stored in glass bottles until it was needed and then placed in a bomb along with gunpowder. It was, evidently, very effective for attacking cities and thought very useful against soldiers in armour because it penetrated the chinks between the plates, causing blistering of the skin. In order that the bombers should not themselves be poisoned, they were ordered to suck licorice as a protection from their own weapons.

Tourist Trap

Several towns have claimed the title of Roughest and Toughest Town in the Wild West, including Abilene and Dodge City. However, according to newspapers and travellers of the 1870s, by far the most dangerous town was Palisade, Nevada. Every single time a train pulled into the station, the passengers stepped out into what seemed to be a full-scale war. The horrified travellers saw gunfights, stabbings, bank robberies and rustlers shooting it out. There were vicious indian attacks, where scores of mounted warriors rode down the main street, gunning down innocent townsfolk – men, women and children. The blood flowed freely and the air was full of the smell of gunsmoke. The terrified travellers rushed to board the train and leave. They didn't give a backward glance, which was a pity because if they had, they would have seen the apparently dead inhabitants of Palisade picking themselves up and going about their normal business. The action-packed scenes of violence were actually cleverly staged to make this quiet backwater into a famous frontier town.

Cannon and Ball

In 1453, the Ottoman Turks used some truly enormous cannons in their attack on Constantinople. The largest fired a ball weighing over 272 kilograms with a diameter of 87.5 cm. A single one of these cannon-balls, fired from a cannon sited 3.4 kilometres away, cut a ship in half. A pair of these giant guns could only be moved by 1,000 soldiers and 70 oxen.

Bungled Invasion

The Spanish Armada sent to attack England in 1588 must have been one of the most badly organised invasions ever. In the first place, the Spanish commander, the Duke of Medina, was not a sailor, hated the sea and suffered from terrible seasickness. He begged King Philip of Spain to choose another commander. In addition to this, the English knew the Spanish fleet was coming and met them with the whole English navy in the Channel, attacking the Spanish ships every centimetre of the way. The Spanish fleet was supposed to collect a Spanish army at the port of Gravelines, but the army had not arrived so the Spanish fleet had to anchor. This allowed the English to send fireships – old ships filled with gunpowder and burning wood – into the Spanish fleet. The Spanish panicked and fled northwards, only to run into a terrible storm which scattered their fleet and wrecked many ships. When the battered Armada limped back to Spain, it had lost 45 of its ships and 27,000 soldiers and sailors.

Kill or Cure

Ever since the dawn of time, people have fallen ill, been injured and suffered pain. When this happened, the sick turned to their local magician, shaman or medicine man. These people still exist, but nowadays we call them doctors. For most of history, doctors did not have the foggiest notion what caused disease, let alone any idea how to cure it. But they found that by sounding confident and charging huge amounts of money, they could give the illusion that they knew what they were doing. They administered a wide range of weird 'cures' – many of which killed their patients. Any successes they had were generally achieved by accident or through luck, rather than by skill. Any patients they killed were rarely in a position to complain very loudly.

Take a Deep Breath

We now know that the plague called the Black Death which came to Europe in 1347 was the Bubonic Plague, spread by fleas which lived on black rats. At the time, many people thought the plague was spread by 'bad air' and believed that they could protect themselves from the diseased air by sniffing strong smells – the stronger the better! Many sniffed bunches of pungent herbs. Others crouched for hours on end over cess-pits, dung-pits and toilets, inhaling deeply.

Bladder Bother

Samuel Pepys, the famous diarist, had a stone the size of a tennis ball removed from his bladder. As was the practice in the 1600s, the operation was performed by a doctor with no anaesthetic, using an unsterilized knife and with unwashed hands. The usual survival rate for this surgery was about one in 20. It is no wonder that Pepys submitted to the operation only when he had been driven nearly mad with the pain of the stone. From that time, every March 26th on the anniversary of his operation, Pepys raised his wine glass and toasted the stone, which he kept in a bottle.

Wriggly Remedy

A popular cure for the gout in the eighteenth century was to apply live earthworms to the affected part. When the worms died and began to smell, it was time to take them off!

Leg of Lamb

One of the earliest cases of transplantation must be the operation performed on a woman from Kazakhstan in Central Asia in about 300 BC. Her left foot had been amputated and replaced with two bones taken from a ram. Apparently the leg had healed and the girl survived. Ancient Egyptians made replacement legs hundreds of years before this, but these limbs were simply cosmetic. They were made of reeds and mud, and were designed only to replace the lost limbs of corpses to allow the dead to go whole into the afterlife.

Dental Drivel

Pliny the Elder, an Ancient Roman encyclopedist, wrote that toothache could be cured by dropping into the ear olive oil in which earthworms had been boiled. He also wrote that scratching aching gums with the tooth of a man who had died violently would cure the pain, and that a frog strapped to the jaw would make loose teeth firm again. Let's hope he never suffered from toothache!

Ant Antidote

In ancient times in many parts of the world, including India and South America, a surgeon never attempted to sew up large cuts. Instead he used nature's remedy. He placed giant ants along the wound and used their jaws to clamp it shut. The surgeon then cut off the bodies of the ants, leaving only the heads with the jaws still clipping the wound shut. These strange stitches stayed in place until the wound healed.

43

Cranky Cure

Dr Kellogg, the inventor of Corn Flakes, had some strange ideas about health which he put into operation during the 1880s at his clinic in Battle Creek, USA. People who were underweight had to stay in bed day and night where they were forced to eat up to 26 meals a day. To make sure that they did not burn up a single calorie, the patients were not allowed to take any physical exercise – even their teeth were brushed by nurses.

'Orrible ointment

In about 3 BC, the founder of modern medicine, the Greek doctor Hippocrates, wrote that if you boiled the head of a hare and three mice, then rubbed the result on the gums, it would cure your bad breath. Any takers?

Zulu Brew

The Zulus had a taste for powerful medicines. These were usually made from the organs and secretions of animals which were prepared and cooked by the witch doctor. Medicines were made into ointments. A Zulu warrior who killed an enemy wanted to avoid any bad luck which might follow the death. He had to be freed of the victim's evil spirit by a special potion. The witch doctor killed a cow and removed dung from its entrails. The dungwas boiled with the cow's gall bladder to make a very strong-tasting liquid! The warrior drank some of this and spread the rest over his body. Then he waited a short while until he was violently sick. The Zulus believed that evil spirits were flushed out of the body along with the vomit.

Nasty Neck Ache

The last public hanging in Britain took place in 1862 in Cornwall. After John Doidge had been executed, two women arrived at the jail asking to be touched by the dead man's hand. This was believed to be a certain cure for a sore neck!

Gallstone Grenade

In May 1980, a Chinese surgeon used a miniature bomb to break up a gallstone in a 40-year-old patient. The doctor and a bomb expert performed more than 100 experiments before the operation to get exactly the right dosage of explosives. Then the bomb was inserted into the patient's gall bladder and detonated. The patient reported that he felt only a slight vibration followed by a numbing sensation.

Just Making Sure...

Many people in the eighteenth century were terrified of premature burial. Hannah Beswick of Manchester took this fear a little further than most. When she died in 1758, she left instructions for her body to be preserved for 100 years. She also left a large legacy to her doctor, on condition that he made regular visits to check that she had not recovered unexpectedly. The doctor must have found the visiting a bit tedious so to make examinations easier, he brought her body to his own home and kept her inside his grandfather clock. When the doctor finally died, Hannah was put into a museum. Finally in 1868, when everyone was sure that she really was dead, Hannah was buried.

Brain Drain

We know that Stone Age peoples, Ancient Egyptians and Incas all did brain operations. These involved slicing off parts of the skull to reveal the brains below – a type of operation called trepanning. Scientists now believe that one of the main reasons why this was done was to remove tapeworm larvae from the skull. Perhaps anything, even a brain operation with no anaesthetic or antiseptics and no sharp steel instruments, was preferable to the agony that hungry tapeworms in the brain could cause.

45

Medieval Whip-Round

One group of people in the Middle Ages believed that the Black Death was a punishment sent from God. They believed that if they could prove how truly sorry they were for all their sins, God might forgive them and keep them safe from the plague. These people, who were known as 'flagellants', flogged themselves and each other with metal-studded whips. When a group of flagellants arrived in town everyone turned out to see the fun. Wearing only linen kilts, the flagellants stood in a circle chanting hymns and thrashing each other in time to the singing. Each flagellant tried to outdo his or her neighbour in suffering, and the blood flowed freely. This show could be repeated three times a day and was entirely free for the spectators.

Just a Wee Drop

The Ancient Chinese were pioneers in making medicines from human urine which they evaporated in pans. It is only in the last 70 years that doctors in the West have started to copy this technique to produce large amounts of human hormones that are proving useful in treating a wide variety of illnesses.

Worming Your Way into Favour

During the nineteenth century in the USA, travelling medicine shows went from town to town, selling bogus patent cures to trusting audiences. One trick was for someone posing as a doctor to arrive at a town, seek out the thinnest inhabitant and inform him that he had the worst case of tapeworm infection the 'Doctor' had ever seen. The Doctor would then give the sufferer a miracle cure of a large capsule and a bottle of medicine. The treatment was free, on condition that the patient came to the medical lecture the next day, bringing the result of the treatment in a jar. What the patient did not realise was that the capsule contained a one-metre long imitation rubber tapeworm which was quickly expelled by the strong laxative contained in the medicine bottle. The whole audience at the medicine show the next day were greatly impressed with the apparent miracle cure given to someone they knew well, and rushed to buy the doctor's products. The doctor always managed to retrieve the tapeworm before it could be examined and so was able to use it again and again.

Power Shower

During the 1800s, water cures became very popular. At a clinic in Malvern, there was a famous 'Rain Bath'. This was a shower run off a very high water tank to make the water shoot out of the shower heads with great force. The jets of water were directed at the painful area. However, so great was the power of this shower that patients were advised to wear a strong hat to protect their heads from injury. One nervous lady took a chair into the shower and stood on it, presumably to be nearer the shower head. She may have hoped that by reducing the height the water had to fall, the shower would be more gentle. In fact, the power of the water simply smashed the chair! A gentleman went into the shower in winter, not realising that an unseen icicle had formed on the shower head. When the shower was turned on, the force of the water propelled the icy spike into his back faster than a speeding bullet. The poor man was so numb with cold, he did not realise that he had been wounded until he came out of the shower.

Strange Customs

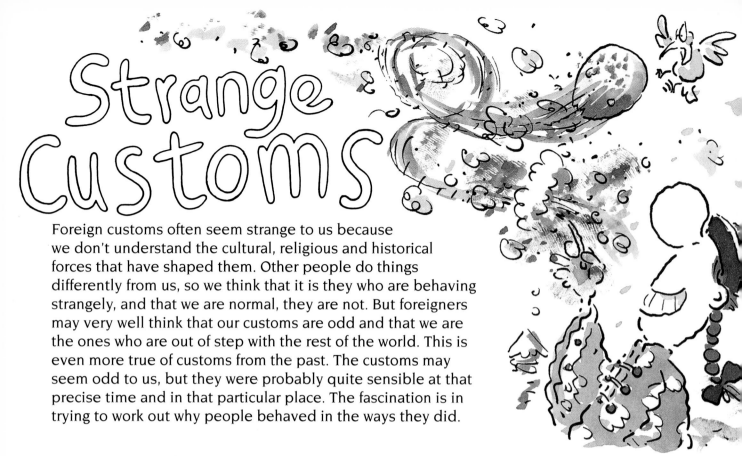

Foreign customs often seem strange to us because we don't understand the cultural, religious and historical forces that have shaped them. Other people do things differently from us, so we think that it is they who are behaving strangely, and that we are normal, they are not. But foreigners may very well think that our customs are odd and that we are the ones who are out of step with the rest of the world. This is even more true of customs from the past. The customs may seem odd to us, but they were probably quite sensible at that precise time and in that particular place. The fascination is in trying to work out why people behaved in the ways they did.

Revered Reptiles

Crocodiles were considered sacred in Ancient Egypt. They were kept in sacred lakes and tended by priests. Some of the animals even wore golden earrings and had bracelets on their forelegs.

Fitness Fanatic

Every spring, Frederick the Great, emperor of Germany, paraded his army along with a regiment of doctors. To clear out his system, every soldier was given a drink to make him vomit and medicine to make him go to the toilet. After this, each soldier had a vein cut and blood drawn off. Frederick believed that this 'spring clean' would keep his soldiers ready for anything.

Pyrotechnic Playthings

Two thousand years ago, Chinese children would put dried plant stems inside empty eggshells. When the stems, which burned easily, were set alight, the eggshells flew away.

High as a Kite

Although the Wright Brothers are credited with being the first people to fly a heavier-than-air machine, people in China flew hundreds of years earlier using kites. Marco Polo records that when a Chinese ship at the time of Kublai Khan was about to start a voyage, the crew would find a drunken or stupid sailor and strap him to a large kite. The kite was then flown. If it flew high and well, everyone was sure that the voyage would be a success. If the kite fell from the sky, the crew would not set sail that day – least of all the sailor on the kite who was probably killed by the fall or drowned before he could be pulled back on board.

Mummy's Little Pets

Everyone knows that the Ancient Egyptians mummified their dead so that they would live again in the afterlife. They also mummified animals that they considered sacred. A tomb near Karnak contained 500,000 mummified cats. A tomb near Saqqara contains the mummified remains of 500 baboons and five million birds. Nearby are the ruins of what must be the first factory farm. Here Egyptian priests reared huge numbers of birds, particularly ibis and hawks. The birds were eventually killed, mummified and sold to faithful worshippers to be put into the tombs of their relatives. Archaeologists also found the ruins of a pottery factory and thousands of tiny pottery coffins, each one containing a single shrew – presumably spirit prey for the spirit hawks that the spirit humans carried with them into the afterlife.

Weird People

History is littered with the most peculiar people – mad, bad and worse. One of the most intriguing was Count Dracula. Yes, there was a real-life Dracula, although he was not actually a vampire. He was a fifteenth-century Slavic prince, Vlad Tepes, also known as Count Vlad Dracul, or Vlad the Impaler. Dracul means 'dragon' and 'devil' in Romanian. Prince Vlad earned this nickname because of his ruthless treatment of enemies. He truly was 'Mad Vlad and dangerous to know'! The tales of Dracula's cruelty have become folk tales used to scare children all over Eastern Europe. Some of the less gruesome ones are included in this chapter. We think of a vampire being killed by a stake driven through the heart. You will soon see that in Dracula's day, stakes were used for quite a different purpose and were plunged into quite a different part of the anatomy! But, although Dracula is really the star of this chapter, you will find plenty of other eccentrics here as well.

Armour-Plated Aussie

Ned Kelly was an Australian horse thief and robber. When the police caught up with Kelly and his gang, the bandit leader was wearing home-made armour. This weighed over 40 kilograms – nearly twice as much as the armour worn by medieval knights. In fact it was so heavy that Ned could hardly lift his gun to shoot! Even so, the armour must have been effective because, in spite of 28 bullet wounds, Ned was the only member of his gang to survive the final shoot-out. He recovered fully from his wounds, only to be hanged five months later.

Good Doggy!

Henry Egerton, eighth Earl of Bridgewater, was very fond of dogs and took a dozen or so with him wherever he went. Every day he dined with his canine companions sitting in seats around the table with napkins round their necks. The dogs, who were dressed in fashionable made-to-measure clothes, were expected to behave with dignity and eat from plates. The Earl talked to the dogs and listened indulgently to what they had to say! But if any dog forgot itself for a moment and stopped behaving like a perfect gentleman, it was ordered to leave the table until it had learned better manners!

Minding their Manners

Count Dracula hated Turks. On one occasion when receiving 55 Turkish ambassadors, he was insulted when, following their own customs, they did not remove their turbans. Determined to get his own back, Count Dracula pretended to be delighted with this practice and told the Turks that he would like to help them keep their hats on forever. He called for a hammer and then, one by one, nailed the ambassadors' hats to their heads.

Raising the Stakes

Count Dracula earned the nickname of Vlad the Impaler because of his love of executing his enemies by impaling them on sharp wooden stakes. He killed thousands of people in this way. He is reputed to have impaled 20,000 men, women and children after capturing the town of Amlas. Stories tell how, before the prisoners were hoisted on stakes, Dracula strode among them, 'cutting them up like cabbages' with his sword.

Count Dracula liked to remind his subjects how ruthless he was by letting them watch his enemies being impaled. The smell of blood, guts and worse must have been overpowering. On one occasion, a particular lord asked Dracula if the spectators could move away from the sickening smell. Instantly, Dracula ordered his servants to bring a stake that was three times as long as normal. Ignoring the pleas of the unfortunate lord, Dracula ordered him to be impaled at once. 'Is the smell any better up there?' shouted Dracula as the lord was hoisted high.

Solving the Unemployment Problem

Fed up with the large number of beggars in the streets, Count Dracula invited dozens to a feast. While they were eating, he ordered his soldiers to set fire to the house and burned them all alive.

Curious Cleric

Robert Hawker, Vicar of Morwenstow in 1835, was a great eccentric and joker. One night when the moon was full, Robert perched on a rock wearing an oilskin tail and a wig made of seaweed, pretending to be a mermaid. A crowd, attracted by the mermaid's raucous singing, soon gathered. Then, with a final performance of the national anthem, the mermaid dived into the sea and vanished. Robert continued for many more years as vicar, visiting his parishioners wearing a yellow blanket, riding on a mule and carrying his trusty pet pig!

Keeping Himself to Himself

William Scott, fifth Duke of Portland, was such a shy man that he organised his life so he would never have to meet anyone. The Duke issued his orders by letter and allowed only his valet to see him. Workmen dug a maze of tunnels and underground rooms under his house, Welbeck Abbey, so he could move around unseen. The Duke seldom went above ground and usually did so at night. He was accompanied by a servant, carrying a lantern, who had to walk ten metres in front of his master. Workers on the estate were instructed to ignore the Duke and, if they accidentally met him, to 'treat him as if he were a tree'.

A Long Lie-in

Florence Nightingale became a legend through nursing the sick and comforting the dying during the Crimean War. However, her fantastic nursing work seems to have tired her out. On returning to England she went to bed and didn't get up for 54 years! Although bedridden, Florence continued to work. She organised the Army Medical Department, improved sanitation in India and founded a nurses' training school – all from the comfort of her bed. She wrote several books, including one on sinks. She was visited in her bedroom by cabinet ministers, ambassadors, generals and doctors, all seeking her advice. Many people thought that Florence wasn't ill at all, but just suffering from hypochondria.

Ungenerous Spirit

During the eighteenth century, John Overs made a fortune operating a ferry service across the Thames but, being very mean, he spent as little money as he could. He fed his servants mouldy bread and rotten meat. His final money-saving wheeze was to pretend to be dead. He thought that the servants would go into mourning and would fast – saving him a day's food. But, as he lay wrapped in a sheet, he heard them celebrating the death of their skinflint master! When he realised they were planning a feast, he sat up to protest. Terrified by the sheeted apparition and thinking it to be a ghost, one of the servants struck John on the head and killed him.

I Want to be Alone

In Victorian times, James Lucas, the 'Mad Hermit of Hertfordshire', loved his mother so much that when she died he personally embalmed her body and put it in a glass coffin in the living room. He guarded the coffin for thirteen weeks until police broke in and took it away.

When they had gone, James, who was apparently terrified of being attacked, barricaded himself in. He turned his house into a fortress and spent most of his time in the kitchen wearing sackcloth and ashes. He cleared out all the furniture and slept on a pile of cinders. He never cut his nails or combed his hair. Gradually his body became covered with a thick layer of grease and grime. Although he looked a terrifying sight, people often came to visit the Mad Hermit and chat with him through the kitchen window. One visitor described James as the dirtiest man in England.

Balloony Loony

Early balloonists couldn't decide on the best way to make their balloons rise. Some favoured hydrogen gas. Others promoted hot air. In 1785, Frenchman François de Rozier decided to become the first man to fly across the English Channel. He chose a hydrogen balloon but then, at the very last minute, thought that perhaps he would be wise to use hot air. Finally, in an agony of indecision, he decided to use both at the same time. Unfortunately, when he lit the fire to create the hot air, the flames ignited the highly flammable hydrogen gas inside the balloon's envelope. De Rozier and his balloon exploded in the first balloon disaster.

Royal Rascals

Royal roguery is always so much more interesting than the criminality of commoners. Although we can all behave badly from time to time, somehow the bad behaviour of royalty always seems much worse than the sinning of ordinary folk. When kings and queens go bad, they seem to corrupt half their subjects as well, and the more powerful the monarch, the worse the consequences can be. Royal villainy can be practised on a very grand scale indeed.

Unwelcome Guests

Soon after Tsar Peter the Great of Russia came to the throne, he went on a fact-finding tour of Europe, travelling incognito. During his visit to England, Peter and his companions stayed in a house in London where they amused themselves in the evenings by drinking and horseplay. After the Russian Royals left, the horrified owners discovered that all their curtains and bed linen were fouled, their paintings had all been vandalised, 50 chairs had been chopped up for firewood, 300 window panes had been smashed, and the floors were covered with grease, ink and vomit.

A Man of his Word

Tamerlane the Great, the cruel Mongol leader, promised the citizens of Sivas in Turkey that if they surrendered he would not spill one drop of their blood. When the citizens did surrender, Tamerlane kept his word, in a manner of speaking. The 4,000 Armenian soldiers who had defended the city were burned alive. The Christians were either strangled or drowned in the moat. And the children were herded into a field to be trampled to death by the Mongol cavalry.

Ferocious Pharaoh

Amenhotep II, Pharaoh of Egypt in about 1427 BC, loved a good fight. He always led his soldiers into battle and his bloodcurdling war cries struck fear into the hearts of his enemies. He personally beheaded the chiefs of all the tribes he defeated, and returned with their bodies hanging upside down from the bows of his ships. Judging by the accounts of his deeds, Amenhotep was something of a superman. He could row six times as far as 200 men and beat anyone in a drinking contest. We also know from his mummified remains that he suffered from chronic toothache and probably died from infection caused by his bad teeth. Could this be what made him so wild?

Emperor Joshua

One of the least-known US presidents was His Imperial Highness Emperor Joshua I. A businessman who fell on hard times, Joshua Norton appointed himself US President in 1859. For 21 years he went about San Francisco in a magnificent uniform, carrying a large sword or, in wet weather, a Chinese umbrella. The citizens bowed or curtsied to him, and gave him free meals and clothes. Joshua passed many laws which everyone ignored, including one abolishing Congress (the US parliament). Emperor Joshua spent his days inspecting drains, checking public transport, discussing the crime rate with police, and taxing shopkeepers. When he died, over 10,000 people filed past his coffin to pay their respects.

Handsome Henry Tudor

When Henry VIII died in 1546 at the age of 55, he was not a pretty sight. He weighed over 182 kilograms. His horribly swollen legs were covered in pus-filled ulcers which had to be dressed several times a day and gave off a loathsome stink. He gasped for breath all the time, and his face was usually purple as if he were in a violent rage – which, of course, he often was.

Rotten Russian Ruler

In 1570, Tsar Ivan IV led his army to punish the citizens of Novgorod. They built a stockade round the city so no one could get out. First came the torture. Most citizens suffered caning on the soles of their feet, or removal of fingernails, tongues, hands, ears and even ribs with red-hot pincers. After the torture came the executions – roasting, impaling, being dragged behind horses, or scorched to death on man-sized metal pans. Many were drowned, their bodies choking the icy waters of the River Volkhov. The most important citizens were given even more horrific public executions in Moscow. These ghastly activities were personally supervised by Ivan and helped to earn this cruellest and maddest Tsar, the nickname 'Ivan the Terrible'.

Odds and Ends

In any collection there are always a few items which don't fit in quite so well. This chapter contains all the incidents and people which couldn't be shoe-horned into one of the other chapters, but were too interesting or too horrible to be left out.

Passenger Pigeon Poop Problem Passes Away Permanently

The North American passenger pigeon used to be one of the most numerous birds on Earth and made up one-third of the bird population of North America. One naturalist described a flock that took three days to pass overhead, estimating that they were passing at a rate of 300 million birds an hour. The roar of their wings could be heard 9.6 kilometres away. Naturally the droppings from these birds became a problem, and Americans began to hunt them down. They shot and poisoned the pigeons. They fed them alcohol-soaked grain and clubbed them to death as they staggered around drunkenly. They even suffocated roosting birds with smoke from fires. The numbers of pigeons reduced rapidly. On 1st September 1914, the very last passenger pigeon, called Martha, died in captivity. Her body was preserved in ice, then stuffed and displayed in a collection of rare birds.

Mathematical Error

The Greek mathematician Archimedes was killed at the age of 75 while he was working out a mathematical problem. In 212 BC, Archimedes' home town of Syracuse was attacked by Romans. The Roman commander, Marcellus, had given strict orders that Archimedes was to be spared. But when the soldiers burst into Archimedes' house, the great man was completely engrossed in a maths problem. He waved an arm impatiently to shoo the soldiers away. One, thinking he was being attacked himself, stabbed the Greek to death.

Papal Inspiration

Medieval doctors were unable to cure the Black Death. Many people turned instead to the Church. But individual prayer and worship did not seem any more effective against the disease. In 1348, Pope Clement VI hit on the idea that perhaps joint worship might do the trick. He called upon the people to make a mass pilgrimage to Rome. More than 1,250,000 pilgrims responded. Unfortunately, packed together in Rome, they soon fell victim to the plague, which spread among them like wildfire. Less than one-tenth of the pilgrims lived to return home.

A Rum Coffin

When Admiral Nelson was killed at the battle of Trafalgar, his body was placed in a cask of spirits and brought back to England. Legend has it that the sailors who brought him home drank the cask dry in his memory.

Going off the Rails

In 1885, the railway between St Louis and Jefferson City was completed. To celebrate this and to open the line, a special train carrying 200 passengers set out from St Louis to make the first journey. The bands played and people cheered. Unfortunately, the train never arrived in Jefferson City because someone had forgotten to mention that a bridge carrying the line over the river Gasconade had not been finished!

Time's Up!

A year is actually 365 days, 6 hours, 48 minutes and 46 seconds long. The odd hours, minutes and seconds can cause a bit of confusion with the calendar because the year just won't divide up equally. The Aztecs got round the problem by saving up the odd bits and then, every now and then, having a period which they called the 'Nothing Days' when they hid indoors because they thought the world might end. These inconvenient left-over hours, minutes and seconds have been a problem throughout history. In Europe in 1582, Pope Gregory XIII ordered that the calendar should be changed because it had got out of step with real time. The adjustment led to the loss of 11 whole days. This caused uproar in some places, particularly among those people whose birthdays and other important personal anniversaries simply vanished into thin air. In fact some countries, such as Britain, refused to adopt this newfangled calendar until 1752!

Dead Interesting

One of the first theme parks must have been a complex of tunnels built by the Ancient Romans near the island of Capri. This seems to have been constructed to represent the entrance to hell itself. Before its closure by Emperor Augustus in about the year 0, this Oracle of the Dead was a popular tourist attraction. Roman tourists were given guided tours through passages lit by flickering torches, by priests dressed in black robes. They even visited the river Styx, across which the dead were supposed to travel to reach Hades, carried by the boatman Charon.

We Are Not Amused

The Ancient Chinese were very fond of fireworks. One type, called a 'ground rat', shot along the ground before exploding. 'Water rats' worked in a similar way but they were equipped with tiny skis so they could whizz across water. On one occasion the Empress-Mother Kung Sheng was terrified when, at a firework display, a ground rat shot along the ground towards the throne. Fearing that it might shoot up her skirt, Kung Sheng leaped to her feet and, gathering her clothes tightly round her, stopped the celebrations. The officials responsible for the display were arrested.

Napoleonic Gnashers

At the time of the battle of Waterloo in 1815, it was customary for the victorious soldiers to loot the bodies of the dead. Apart from weapons, items of uniform, money and jewellery, teeth were highly prized. In those days, false teeth were often carved from ivory. But dentists could make more realistic sets of dentures from the teeth of dead people. For years after the battle, dentures were known as 'Waterloo Teeth'.

Did You Know...

…that gunpowder was invented almost completely by accident? The Chinese inventor mixed the correct recipe using saltpetre, sulphur and charcoal as he experimented to find a miracle medicine for longer life. Apparently the resulting explosion not only burned him, but destroyed his house as well.

…that drilling for oil began over 800 years ago in the Middle East? Some archaeologists believe that the ancient city of Sodom, mentioned in the Bible as being destroyed by God, was actually wiped out by a firestorm. This was caused by cooking fires igniting petroleum gases given off by nearby oil deposits. The exploding gases rained boiling oil on the city, destroying all life within its walls.

…. that King George II died on the toilet during an attack of chronic constipation?

…that when Henry II died in France in July 1189, his corpse smelled so bad in the summer heat that his servants were not able to take the body to a state funeral. In fact they could carry the corpse only 17.6 km (11 miles) before the sickening stench forced them to bury it hurriedly.

…that Adolf Hitler actually did have only one testicle (the right one) due to a birth defect?

…that the artist Francisco de Goya was probably killed by his own paint? Goya mixed his own paints, and to do this he ground up, amongst other things, mercury and lead – two very poisonous metals which accumulated in his body and slowly killed him (however, he did manage to live to the age of 82).

…that when doctors who caused the death of the wounded President Garfield, through their bungling and unhygenic treatment, submitted a bill of $85,000 for their services, the US Senate agreed to pay them $10,000 only, and that was on condition that they publicly admitted their mistakes?

…that in 1484, Pope Innocent VIII called on the Church to stamp out witchcraft? All over Europe, people responded with enthusiasm. As many as one million people, mostly women, were tortured and executed – usually by being burned alive. They were all certainly innocent.

… that Henry VIII created a record for an English king by ordering, during the course of his reign, the execution of an estimated 72,000 of his subjects?

… that the last person in Britain to be pressed to death was Henry Cook, a Stratford shoemaker, convicted of robbery?

...that in 1880, 28 tons of mummified cats were sent from Egypt to Liverpool, where they were ground up and sold as fertiliser?

...that thousands of years before the building of the Suez Canal, the Ancient Egyptians built a canal which connected the Mediterranean Sea to the Red Sea?

... that the first skier was a Norwegian of around 2,500 BC?

... that in 1395 a 15-year-old girl named Liedwi, who was skating, was knocked down by another skater and badly hurt? Liedwi was so shocked that she went into a convent and devoted her life to religious work. She became the patron saint of skaters.

.... that Roman ice cost more than wine? The Emperor Elagabalus once had a mountain of ice and snow built in his garden on a hot summer day as an early form of air-conditioning. It cost him a small fortune.

... that tobacco was introduced to Europe from America by Sir Walter Raleigh? Of course you did! Then how do you explain that the mummy of Pharaoh Ramesses II of Egypt who died over 3,000 years ago was stuffed with old tobacco leaves?

... that the world's oldest counterfeit money is a copy of a silver coin from Greece made over 2,500 years ago?

... that the first paper money introduced by the Chinese in about AD 800 was called 'flying money' because the wind could easily blow it away?

... that Pharaoh Thutmoses III once made a single offering in the Temple of Amun at Thebes of 13.5 tonnes of gold worth about £10 million in today's prices?

... that the Aztec Emperor, Montezuma, had a large zoo? One of the prize exhibits was a collection of rattlesnakes.

... that an Ancient Greek inventor called Hero invented a simple steam engine? You probably did. But did you know that he also invented automatically opening temple doors and an automatic miniature theatre in which an ingenious arrangement of weights and pulleys operated mechanical puppets? Apparently the theatre showed a complete performance of a play about the Trojan War.

... that during the 800s the Chinese made and used paper armour? This armour, which was made of many layers of folded mulberry paper, was actually better than iron armour of the time and gave almost total protection from arrows. The invention of more powerful crossbows (and, presumably, matches!) eventually made paper armour less useful.

... that hand grenades were first used in war during the Crusades? They were basically egg-shaped pottery vessels filled with petroleum.

Index